My Mom is Dying

A Child's Diary

Written by
Jill Westberg McNamara

Illustrated by
David LaRochelle

Augsburg
MINNEAPOLIS

To all the children who read this book

exercising
MY Mom
This is good
YES
We're making a salad with fruit.

September 15

God?

Are you listening? This is Kristine and I need to talk to you.

My mom is dying. At least that's what Dad told me... but I don't believe him. She's my mom and she can't die. She's way too nice. Besides, how can she die? She takes such good care of herself. She eats tons of fruit and vegetables and she jogs or rides her bike almost every day. You should see her swimming up at the lake. She's terrific!

But Dad says she's sick. And she's getting sicker. And she's going to die.

<u>She can't die! I need her.</u>

<u>Please</u>, God, don't let her die.

September 18

Mom had to go back into the hospital because she couldn't stand up. An ambulance came to get her.

I know she's real sick. I've known that for a while. But the medicines were supposed to make her better....

I'm scared. Could she really be dying? What would life be like without her?

I need your help, God.

All the neighbors ↑ are watching

September 23

Dear God,

I'm glad I have you to talk to. Mom and Dad spend so much time answering my questions, but it seems that when I crawl into bed more questions pop into my head. I think about Mom all the time.

I know I can't catch what she has or anything like that, but I wonder about death:
    What is it like?
    Will it hurt?
How long will Mom live? Mom and Dad say that they don't know these answers either. They say that we ought to have as much fun as we can for now, because that's the best we can do.

September 25

Mom came home from the hospital today. You'd think that would make me happy, but it doesn't. I know I love her, but at the same time I'm mad at her. I feel really mixed up.

I did an awful thing today and I don't know why. Mom asked me to run downstairs and get the newspaper. I said, "NO WAY!" I also said it was nicer here without her because Dad didn't make me work so much.

I didn't mean to say that. Somehow it just came out. Why should I be mad at Mom? She can't help that she's sick. It's not like she wants to be sick. Help me understand. I'm so confused.

September 26

   I hope Mom knows I'm sorry that I was mean to her last night. I know I should have gone in her room and said, "I'm sorry," but I couldn't do it. So I drew a picture of me holding her hand. I wrote "I love you" above it.

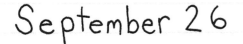

Then I knelt outside Mom's door and coaxed Smudge (our dog) to carry the paper to her. It was soggy when it reached Mom, but she smiled.

October 1

Mom has a hospital bed in her room. It's sort of fun because you can crank it up and down. We also have nurses that come to our house to check on her so that she won't have to keep going back to the hospital. The nurses are pretty nice. Today they let me help take her blood pressure. My job was to hold onto the black rubber bulb and pump it up. It was neat. Maybe I can do it again.

stethoscope

← (I got to use this too!)

←thermometer

lots of medicine

October 15

God,

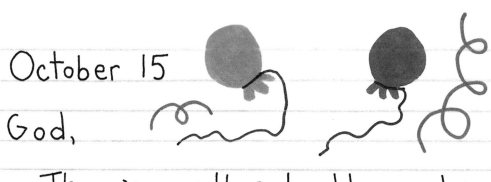

There's a mother-daughter party at school on Friday night with ice-cream sundaes and games and everything. Not every mother can go. Heather's mom lives too far away so for sure she won't be there. But I still wish my mom could go. It's not fair.

Dad says that Grandma or Aunt Michelle would take me, but I don't want to go with them. I want to go with Mom. What a **LOUSY** deal.

COME TO THE
mother *games*
daughter
ICE CREAM party! *fun!*

October 20

Hey God,

    I'm scared. I heard Dad talking on the phone to Grandma last night. He was telling Grandma that he was worried about who would take care of me after school and during vacations. Grandma can't watch me because she already has a job. I sure don't want to go to day care at the Nelson's house. The little kids there are always crying or following you around.

ME AT DAY CARE

If I have to go to day care, I might not be able to play soccer. And who's going to help me with school projects? And my piano practicing?

What's going to happen to us? Why can't you just <u>make Mom better?</u>

WAA!

WAA!

November 3

Sometimes I think about the most horrible things. This morning, during silent reading, my eyes saw the words but I was really wondering about why Mom got sick.

Then I remembered about a year ago, when she was still okay, Mom was exercising in the living room. I was bored, so for fun I was counting how many times I could jump over her. Well, on number twelve I tripped and fell right on top of her. She yelled a little, then grabbed her stomach.

Could that have made her sick? I feel awful about it, but I'm afraid to say anything. Oh God, what if it was my fault?

6, 7, 8, 9...

BE CAREFUL KRISTINE

November 5

The last two days were terrible. My stomach hurt all the time and I could hardly eat. Mostly I just drank apple juice. Today I came home from school before lunch.

I knew I was feeling crummy because I was afraid that I made Mom sick, but I couldn't ask Dad about it. He'd hate me if it was my fault!

Finally I figured out what to do. I called Aunt Michelle. She's real easy to talk to and I knew she wouldn't suspect anything. For awhile I told her about school. Then I asked her if people could get super sick from having someone fall on them. She said that might cause pain or a broken bone, but it wouldn't make them sick like Mom.

You can't believe how much better I felt. I was so relieved that I started to cry. After we hung up I cried some more and then I raced downstairs and ate two bowls of Cheerios. Thanks for Aunt Michelle, God!

November 23

Hey God,

At school today Mrs. Spencer had my whole third grade class make cards for Mom. We were supposed to draw pictures and write about things that make us laugh.

Mom cheered when I hauled that huge bag of cards into her room. We spent the afternoon reading them.

What is purple and flies?

SUPER, GRAPE!

PASTOR MCDONALD!

My kitten wearing a sock!

Peter wrote some dumb jokes. Lisa wrote about the time her minister was at her house and her two lizards jumped on him.

Danny drew pictures of a snow monster he had built. Those snow monster pictures made Mom and me cry because building monsters and forts out of snow is something that we love to do together. We know we won't be able to do it again.

November 28

Today is Thanksgiving. But I don't have anything to be thankful for.

Dinner was awful. I mean the food was okay, but it just wasn't like Thanksgiving used to be. There were fourteen of us and everyone was pretending that nothing was wrong. The grown-ups were saying stuff like how thankful they were that we were all together and that my cousins and I are doing well in school and that Aunt Marie served dinners to some homeless families today. What's so great about that?

Cousin Alicia

Uncle Mike

Mr. Tyler

Grandma

Cousin Teri

Aunt Lisa

Ben

Then grandpa told Mom how terrific she looked. What a joke! I said I was thankful that Thanksgiving only comes once a year. Grandma looked at me real mad like, so I hushed up until dessert.

I'm sorry I was such a pain.

Dad ↓

Mom ↘

Me ↓

Grandpa ↓

Aunt Michelle ↑

Cousin Aaron ↑

Aunt Marie ↑

January 10

God,

The nurses are here almost constantly to take care of Mom. She can't even dress herself. They give her medicine so she doesn't hurt.

My job is to read to her when I get home from school. We used to play cards, but now she's usually too tired to hold the cards. So we read. I remember when Mom used to read these same books to me. Right now we're reading <u>Calvin and Hobbes</u>. That's our favorite.

Oh, God, I think Mom is going to die soon. Why won't you help her? Please help me and Dad understand.

February 2

God,

It finally happened. Mom died today. I was building with my Legos when Dad came downstairs to tell me.

It was real weird when he told me, because I wasn't sad at all. Instead I asked him if it would be okay if I went over to Jacob's house for awhile.

I played with Jacob the rest of the afternoon. You'd think nothing had happened. I knew I should feel sad. I thought maybe there was something wrong with me. But I kept playing because that's what felt right.

Later, at home, I peeked in Mom and Dad's room and saw the empty hospital bed. That started me crying a little. But, you know, when I turned away, I was fine again. I told this to Grandma when she brought supper over. She said not to worry. She said she was having a hard time believing Mom had died too, but it didn't mean she didn't care.

February 5

The memorial service for Mom was today, God. There must have been a hundred people. Some of my friends came and even my teacher, Mrs. Spencer. I didn't know what to say when people told me they were sorry, so I ended up just saying "thank-you" which seemed alright. Some grown-ups hugged me who I didn't want to hug.

During the service my Mom's friend Bill played guitar and sang some of her favorite songs. I don't know how he could sing without crying. I started crying and I felt so dumb because I knew everyone could see me.

At the Memorial Service

People took turns telling nice things about Mom that they wanted everyone to know. Some of the stories were pretty funny. Like when Mom was in college she stuffed her friend's car full of balloons. Mom has a lot of people who love her.

After the memorial service a bunch of people came to the house. Not many people stayed long, which was good because I was real tired.

People gave us all sorts of food and cookies and books and flowers. We sure have great friends. Grandma's going to stay at our house for a few weeks so Dad and I won't have to be alone. I guess we'll do okay.

Dad

Me

At Home

Miss Ngvuen
(our neighbor)

March 8

God, Mom's been dead for over a month now. I go to Brenda's house after school until Dad picks me up. Both of us fix dinner, which is sort of fun. Did you know that food coloring will turn milk or mashed potatoes any color you want? Washing dishes is really boring, but when I help, Dad and I have time to do things together.

Every now and then, when I'm in a store or another crowded place, I think I see Mom. Of course, it always turns out to be someone else - like a woman who might have the same brown hair and that same bright red jacket Mom wore.

I always think I'll find Mom if I look hard enough. Once I even heard her rattling around in the kitchen making Saturday pancakes, but it was only my imagination. How can death be this <u>forever</u>? I can't quite believe that I'll never see her here again.

Sometimes what I do is think about Mom being with you. That helps.

March 20

Dear God,

   It still hurts when I think about Mom. It's like the hurt will never go away. Dad says it might take a long time - maybe a year or two. But he says it will go away or at least not hurt a whole bunch. And he says that because I love her, I'm bound to be a jumble of emotions for awhile: happy, sad, angry, scared, and confused. That's just the way it is when you love someone.

   I still wish Mom wouldn't have died. But I'm glad that she's not sick anymore. Thank you for sending us good friends who care. And thanks for listening, God.

   Love,
      Kristine

NOTES FROM THE AUTHOR

Each of the seventeen journal entries in this book provides material for discussion with children. Some of Kristine's story may spontaneously elicit comments that relate to your children's experiences. If not, I suggest you begin the discussion with a question.

A good starter question could focus on Kristine. For example, "What was Kristine feeling?" Or it might focus on the reader, "Remember when you were so angry that you _____ ?"

Continue the discussion of each journal entry based on the comments and questions that accompany it. They will provide background for the subject and help you shape the direction of your communication.

Jill Westberg McNamara

September 15

Denial is an early reaction in the grief process. The news of death is too overwhelming to face. Kristine's mother has always been there for her. Kristine can't imagine life without her. She can think of many reasons why her mom can't die: "she eats right, she jogs, she's terrific." Even after Kristine "believes" her mother's diagnosis, it might take a while longer before it "registers" or becomes "real" to her.

September 18

In this conversation with God, the reality of her mother's illness is beginning to sink in. With this gradual awareness come questions such as, "What will my life be like?" Once the true awareness of death hits, it might again fade from time to time. You can talk with children about what it felt like for them when they found out their father or mother was dying. Did they believe it? Were they sad? Were they scared? What did they do to keep from thinking about it all of the time?

September 23

Here Kristine voices some of her questions about death. Emphasize to your children the importance of asking questions. Know that it is okay for you not to have all the answers. What other questions do your children have?

This might be a good opportunity to discuss your beliefs about death with your children.

September 25

Kristine is angry and confused. These emotions are part of the grief process. After blurting out rather harsh words to her mother she is angry with herself.

Kristine's anger is typical; her world is going to be radically altered. In this instance her anger caught her off guard and surfaced at an inopportune time. Discuss similar fits of rage that have happened either to you or your children. What was the real cause? How can we deal with the anger after it explodes? What are some constructive ways of expressing anger? Who can we turn to for help?

September 26

Saying "I'm sorry" can be very difficult, but there is more than one way to apologize. Kristine uses a picture. Discuss other ways to say "I'm sorry."

October 1

Kristine tells God about the medical routine at her house. What happens or will happen in your situation, and how can children participate in that process?

October 15

Here is more anger and frustration as the reality becomes clearer. It *is* "a lousy deal" and that should not be denied. Comparing children's lives to others or saying, "It's not so bad" might only evoke more anger.

When you learn what occasions make children angry, acknowledge them. You needn't try to make it artificially better for them. They want to know that you understand their feelings. Then they are able to move on from there.

October 20

Kristine overhears that her father is worried about the future. Kristine, naturally, picks up on this concern. She still wishes God would just make it all better.

How might the future be changed for your children? Since they have probably already begun to wonder, this entry might be a good lead-in to discuss the future.

November 3

In trying to answer their own questions about death and dying, children sometimes assume guilt: "What could I have done to prevent this?" "What did I do to cause this?"

Kristine does not feel comfortable talking with her parents about her possible guilt. She is afraid they will confirm that she caused her mother's illness. She doesn't want anyone to find out how horrible she is. This is the type of thinking that we hope to avoid through open discussion, but it might still occur. We must be alert for signs of it because children will try to hide it.

November 5

Kristine is upset because she thinks she might have caused her mother's illness. She has developed physical symptoms: her stomach hurts and she is not able to eat. She is fortunate, though, because she has an aunt she can talk to. Hopefully children reading this will see that if they are scared to go to a parent with a question, there might be others they can ask, like a relative or a teacher. Talk with your children about who these other adults might be.

After talking with her aunt Kristine feels better. If she had not resolved this conflict her symptoms might have worsened. Stress is believed by many to be a major cause of illness and physical symptoms are common during the grieving period. Use this as an illustration for your children on the necessity of sharing their feelings with a trusted adult.

November 23

This entry suggests a way that children's friends can be involved. Cards offer a vehicle for conversation between Kristine and her mother.

November 28

The joy surrounding a holiday like Thanksgiving points up the unhappiness in Kristine's life. Many families who are grieving make a concerted effort to remember what they have to be thankful for in the past as well as the present. It may be bittersweet, but it merits celebration.

January 10

Kristine's mother is too weak to even hold the cards, but through the reading she and Kristine can spend some meaningful time together. What activities would be appropriate in your children's situation?

Kristine also asks God, "Why won't you help?" Many people attempt to answer this, yet ultimately it remains a mystery. It is fine if you cannot provide an answer for children. But regardless of how you handle the discussion, this story still points to God as a source of strength and comfort for Kristine. God can be that for your children too.

February 2

Kristine's reaction to her mother's death is disbelief. While many children will be upset, others are just as likely to go out and play after hearing the news. The death is not a reality for them. Help your children to know that they are not expected to act a certain way, such as stoic or sad. God and you will be there for them no matter what form their expression takes.

February 5

A memorial service is held for Kristine's mother. This entry acknowledges, through Kristine's feelings, that it is okay to be averse to hugging, that it is natural to feel embarrassed if you cry, and that this day can be very tiring. It points out that after a death there can be a lot of support through the thoughts and deeds of friends and family.

March 8

Kristine talks about her life—how it is changed. Her viewpoint is positive. No doubt there are also bad days during which her entry would reflect her anger or frustration with the situation. Ask your children how they think they might feel if their lifestyle changes. What might be hard to adjust to? What would be good about it?

Kristine imagines that she sees her mother at a store and hears her in the kitchen. Let your children know that this too is perfectly normal. Even after they have accepted the reality of death, there will be times when they "forget."

The vision Kristine has of her mother with God is comforting. Share with your children your beliefs about life after death. Some references in the Bible are: Romans 6:4–5, 8–9, 11; Romans 8:11; 1 Corinthians 15:12; and 1 Thessalonians 4:13–14, 16–17.

March 20

Kristine's story is not complete with this final entry, but we leave her on a note of hope and thanks to God for sending friends who care. It is likely that Kristine will go through the grief process again and again. She acknowledges her pain, yet at the same time understands that it will lessen with time.